D1389260

CRACK THE PIRATE CODE

Liam O'Donnell

raintree
a Capstone company — publishers for children

Raintree is an imprint of Capstone Global Library Limited, a company incorporated in England and Wales having its registered office at 264 Banbury Road, Oxford OX2 7DY – Registered company number: 6695582

www.raintree.co.uk
myorders@raintree.co.uk

Edited by Bradley Cole
Designed by Kayla Dohmen
Picture research by Wanda Winch
Production by Katy LaVigne
Originated by Capstone Global Library Ltd
Printed and bound in China

ISBN 978 1 4747 4545 1
22 21 20 19 18 17
10 9 8 7 6 5 4 3 2 1

British Library Cataloguing in Publication Data
A full catalogue record for this book is available from the British Library.

Acknowledgements
We would like to thank the following for permission to reproduce photographs: Alamy Stock Photo: Lebrecht Music and Arts Photo Library, 25; Bridgeman Images: © Look and Learn/Private Collection/Kenneth John Petts, 7, © Look and Learn/Private Collection/Ron Embleton, 13, 21, 23, 29, Peter Newark Historical Pictures/Private Collection/Arthur David McCormick, 9; Capstone: Roger Stewart, 19; Getty Images Inc: Bettmann, 17; iStockphoto: JohnGollop, cover (map top, bottom); Paul Daly, 27; Rick Reeves: rickreevesstudio.com, 5, 11; Shutterstock: Andrey Armyagov, cover (middle), Andrey_Kuzmin, 2-3 background, Antony McAulay, 26, grafvision, cover (right), ilolab, vintage paper texture, Melkor3D, 15, Molodec, maps, Nik Merkulov, grunge background, pingebat, pirate icons, sharpner, map directions to island treasure, Triff, nautical background, TyBy, cover (banner).

CONTENTS

Some words are shown in bold, **like this**. You can find out what they mean by looking in the glossary.

Equal treatment

Pirate ships were crowded and dirty. Pirates were nearly always tired, wet and cold. Why did pirates choose to live like this? Because the Pirate **Code** said that they would all be treated the same. It also promised an equal share in any treasure!

Fact

Ships often had many beetles and rats. These pests carried **diseases** that spread quickly. Sometimes half of a ship's **crew** could die from disease.

Working together

Pirates made their living by stealing. They looked for ships carrying gold, spices, weapons and other gear that they could steal.

But pirates had to work hard to get the treasure. The Pirate **Code** made sure that everyone did his job.

Fact

Even people could be treasure. Pirates sometimes **kidnapped** ship doctors and **carpenters**. They also kidnapped and sold some people as **slaves**.

Rules

Every pirate ship had its own list of rules. Before any man joined, he had to first sign the ship's **code**. He had to swear his **loyalty** over the Bible or an axe. The pirate could then take a share of any stolen treasure.

Fact

Pirate captains asked men if they had wives or families. If they did, they usually weren't allowed to join the **crew**.

Pirates could usually **vote** on where they sailed and what ships to attack. If the **crew** didn't like a captain's idea, they wouldn't do it. Pirate crews also voted on who would be their captain. They could just as easily vote him out!

Fact

While on a job for the British government in 1692, Captain Thomas Tew suggested searching for treasure instead. His crew agreed and they became pirates.

Women pirates

On many ships, the **code** said women were not allowed on board. Many pirates thought women were bad luck.

But some women actually became pirates. Anne Bonny and Mary Read sailed with "Calico" Jack Rackham during the early 1700s. They usually dressed as men.

Fact

Even when their ship was captured in 1720, Bonny and Read continued to fight when all the men hid below **deck**.

Lights out!

Piracy was hard work, and pirates needed their sleep. Many ship rules stated that all candles and lamps had to be put out by eight o'clock at night. This helped to prevent fires and avoided giving away the ship's location to the pirates' enemies.

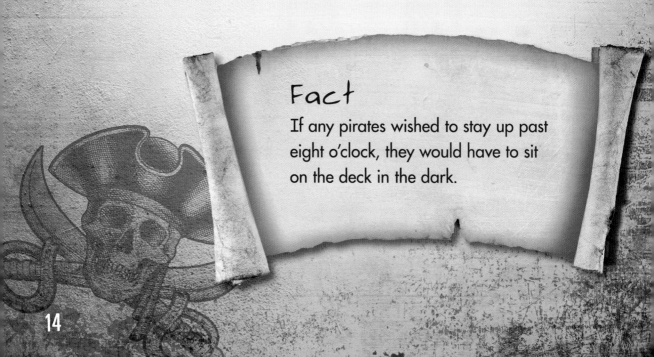

Fact

If any pirates wished to stay up past eight o'clock, they would have to sit on the deck in the dark.

Ready to fight

The Pirate **Code** said that every pirate had to keep his weapons clean. The weapons had to be ready to use. If a pirate let his sword get rusty or his pistol become dirty, he would face **punishment**.

Fact

If a pirate ran away from battle or refused to fight, he would be punished when the fight was over.

Dividing the treasure

According to the **code**, each pirate received a share of treasure based on his job. The more important a pirate's job, the bigger his share of the treasure. The captain usually got two shares. Most crewmembers got only one share.

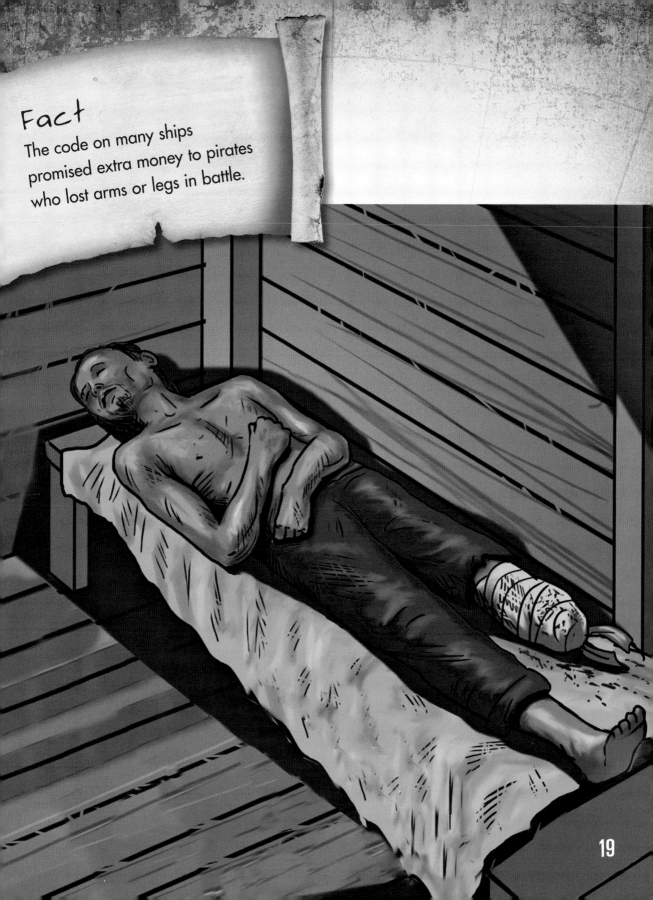

Fact
The code on many ships promised extra money to pirates who lost arms or legs in battle.

Breaking the code

Pirates were feared for their cruel crimes. But pirates often suffered cruel **punishment** as well. Pirates who broke the Pirate **Code** could be **marooned**. A marooned person was left behind on a deserted island, far from any other people. He was given little food or water.

Fact

Pirates who killed a crewmate were forced to do the "Murderer's Swim." First, the pirate was tied to the dead body. Then he was thrown overboard and left to drown.

Pirates were **punished** if they were caught stealing from each other. One punishment was to cut off the thief's nose or ears. Then he was left ashore. Authorities would have likely recognized him as a pirate and punished him for his crimes.

Fact
Walking the plank is the most famous pirate **punishment**. However, it's unlikely that it ever really happened!

Another way to punish a thief was to tie him to the **mainmast** of the ship. The pirate was left without food or water for days. He was often beaten. Sometimes the other pirates circled around him. They jabbed at him with their daggers and swords.

Fact

Pirates would sometimes rub salt or vinegar into the thief's open wounds.

Flogging

Flogging kept pirates from fighting each other or breaking other rules. This **punishment** was done with a special whip called the cat-o'-nine-tails. It had nine ropes attached to a handle. Each rope had knots tied into it. Flogging often caused large, painful cuts.

Fact

Sometimes fishhooks or other sharp objects were tied to the ends of a cat-o'-nine-tails.

Code for success

Some of the **punishments** for breaking the Pirate **Code** were very cruel. But the code made sure pirates lived and worked well together. Without rules, pirates wouldn't have been very successful.

Fact

Sailors were sometimes punished by keelhauling. This involved the sailor being tied with a rope and pulled under the ship. His body was cut by razor-sharp **barnacles**. Most victims drowned.

GLOSSARY

barnacles small shellfish that are covered in very hard shells. They attach themselves to the sides of ships.

carpenter someone who works with wood

code collection of rules that a group of people have to live by

crew group of people who work on a ship

deck upper floor of a ship

deserted empty or abandoned

disease sickness or illness

flogging beating someone with a whip or stick

kidnap capture someone and hold them until you get what you want

location the exact place where someone or something is

loyalty strong feeling of support for other people

mainmast tall post in the centre of a ship to which the main sails are attached

maroon leave someone on a deserted island

punishment action that is carried out against someone to stop them doing something

slave person who is owned by another person. Slaves were forced to work for no money.

vote choice made by a person based on their own views

FIND OUT MORE

Books

Pirate Diary (Diary Histories), Richard Platt (Walker Books, 2014)

Pirate's Handbook, Sam Taplin (Usborne, 2014)

Pirates (Horrible Histories), Terry Deary (Scholastic, 2015)

Pirates' Tools for Life at Sea (Blazers: Pirates!), Cindy Jenson-Elliott (Capstone Press, 2012)

Websites

www.dkfindout.com/uk/history/pirates
Want to know about pirates? This website will tell you all you need to know.

www.rmg.co.uk/discover/explore/life-and-times-pirate
Learn more about the lives of pirates on this website.

Place to visit

National Maritime Museum, Cornwall
Discovery Quay, Falmouth TR11 3QY
Learn all about the lives of people who have worked closely with the sea over the centuries at the National Maritime Museum.

INDEX